HEARTS OF GOLD

Reflections of

EARTH GUARDIAN

Gold Award Girl Scouts

Sheryl M Robinson

Copyright Page

Published by Grow and Share Network, LLC
First Edition, 2026

ISBN: 978-1-972135-01-3

Printed in the United States of America

Books in the Hearts of Gold Series

- *Earth Guardian*
- *STEM*
- *Creative Voice*
- *Inclusion*
- *Health*
- *Advocacy*
- *Community Connector*

Table of Contents

CHAPTER 1

Welcome, Earth Guardians!

Every Big Change Starts with One Small Choice

If you look around your neighborhood, you might notice things that seem small at first: a patch of soil washing away after a storm, a dog that looks nervous at the shelter, or a single bee buzzing near a flower bed. But to an Earth Guardian, these moments aren't small at all — they're signals. They're clues about what the planet needs and how we can help.

Across the country, kids just like you are listening closely to those clues. In this book, you'll meet girls who followed their curiosity, asked brave questions, and took action to protect animals, clean up ecosystems, and bring hope to their communities. Their stories prove something powerful:

You don't have to wait to grow up to make a difference.
You can start right now.

Caring for Creatures Big and Small

Some Earth Guardians focus on saving animals — and not just the fluffy or famous ones. You'll meet girls who saw real needs in the animal world and stepped up:

- Turning Adoption Day into a second chance for overlooked dogs
- Building warm houses for stray cats braving cold nights
- Teaching her community how to treat guide dogs with respect
- Protecting local pets by warning families about hidden dangers

Each of these girls noticed where animals were struggling and asked, "What can I do?"
And then they did it.

Healing the Planet, One Project at a Time

Other Earth Guardians looked to the land, the waterways, and the air around them. They saw erosion, pollution, disappearing pollinators, and rising temperatures — and instead of giving up, they got creative.

These girls:

- Restored a damaged shoreline
- Built hotels for native bees
- Redesigned shower systems to save water
- Cooled down overheated city blocks
- Planted trees to protect future generations
- Challenged companies to reduce plastic pollution

Their projects weren't tiny. Some involved entire neighborhoods, schools, cities, or ecosystems. But they all began with a single idea and one girl willing to try.

What Makes an Earth Guardian Different?

Earth Guardians share three big strengths:

1. **They pay attention.**
   They don't ignore a problem just because it's been there for a long time.
2. **They learn before they act.**
   They talk to experts, research solutions, and make smart plans.
3. **They believe their actions matter.**
   Because they do — even the small ones.

Being an Earth Guardian isn't about perfection. It's about noticing a need and caring enough to respond.

You Belong in This Story Too

As you read these chapters, you'll discover girls who never thought of themselves as scientists, environmentalists, or activists. They were students, dancers, athletes, readers — ordinary kids who saw something that didn't feel right.

Then they changed it.
And you can, too.

Maybe your passion is animals.
Maybe it's pollution.
Maybe it's climate change, recycling, clean water, or preserving local parks.

Whatever makes your heart beat faster — that's where your journey begins.

This book is full of ideas, hope, and examples from girls who cared deeply and acted boldly. Their stories are here to inspire you, guide you, and remind you that:

The planet needs protectors. And you are ready.

CHAPTER 2

Helping Animals Find Their Forever Homes

Shelby Dye — Episode 17

A Problem Hidden in Plain Sight

Have you ever wondered why some pets get adopted almost instantly while others wait… and wait… and wait?

Shelby Dye from Oklahoma had wondered the same thing. She loved animals—she grew up with them, volunteered with them, and earned her Bronze Award helping at her local no-kill shelter, Pets and People. But she didn't understand why certain dogs always seemed to be left behind.

That's when she discovered something heartbreaking:

Black Dog Syndrome (BDS).

Black Dog Syndrome is the pattern where dark-colored dogs (and sometimes cats) are adopted far less often than lighter-colored animals.

- Not because they're less friendly.
- Not because they're less trained.
- Just because of the color of their fur.

Shelby had seen this without realizing it. Her own beloved chocolate Lab fit the description of the dogs being overlooked.

And once she learned the truth, she couldn't unsee it.

The Video That Changed Everything

Shelby was struggling to choose her Gold Award project. She wanted something meaningful—something she cared about. But no ideas felt *right.*

One day, while searching for inspiration, she revisited the Pets and People website. There, she clicked on a video she faintly remembered from years before. It explained Black Dog Syndrome—how many families walk past dark-colored pets without giving them a chance.

As Shelby watched, something inside her cracked open.

"I just started bawling," she said. It hurt to think about good dogs sitting in kennels simply because of how they looked. That sadness quickly turned into determination.

She had found her mission. She would fight for these forgotten animals.

A Cause No One Knew About

Shelby created an ambitious goal:

A yearly adoption day focused on Black Dog Syndrome.

But she immediately hit a major roadblock:

Almost nobody had heard of BDS.

That meant Shelby wasn't just planning an event—she was about to launch a full public awareness campaign. And she had to learn skills she never expected to need:

- How to talk to the media
- How to explain a new idea clearly
- How to motivate people to show up and support her cause

And she had to do it all as a teenager.

Learning to Speak Up

Shelby admitted she didn't start out as a confident communicator. Marketing felt like a giant mountain she wasn't sure she could climb.

But the only way to make Adoption Day successful was to spread the word—far and wide.

She pushed herself.

She spoke with local marketing experts. She emailed different organizations. She contacted television programs asking for airtime.

It was intimidating. It was uncomfortable. But it was necessary.

And finally, something big happened:

Fox News Oklahoma invited her to speak on air.

Standing in front of cameras, talking about a topic so emotional to her, was terrifying. But she did it anyway—and that moment became one of the most important learning experiences of her project.

Shelby discovered that her voice mattered.

Adoption Day Arrives

With her outreach complete, Shelby hosted the first Black Dog Syndrome Adoption Day.

- Families came.
- Shelter animals got attention.
- And dark-colored pets—who were once invisible in their kennels—finally had a moment in the spotlight.

Shelby had turned a quiet problem into a public conversation.

Her work didn't end when the event was over. Her awareness materials and partnerships laid the foundation for the event to continue year after year, ultimately benefiting more animals long after she graduated.

Building to Her Future

Shelby achieved much before starting her project:

- founded her own Girl Scout troop
- served as a youth leader
- sang in her church choir
- played flute and handbells
- performed internationally in the London New Year's Day Parade
- travelled to Ireland, New York, and Italy
- became a drum major

Even though she was busy with all of that, Shelby says her Gold Award meant the most to her.

Why?

Because it taught her:

- How to advocate for something she believes in
- How to convince strangers to care
- How to turn a local problem into a real movement
- How persistence can change lives—human and animal

She learned that a cause doesn't have to be huge to be important.

It just must matter. And if you care enough, you'll find the courage to fight for it.

What You Can Learn from Shelby

1. **Look closer — small problems can hide big truths.**
   Black Dog Syndrome is easy to overlook until someone points it out.
2. **Your voice is stronger than you think.**
   Shelby spoke on television because she believed in her cause.
3. **Learning new skills can unlock new opportunities.**
   Marketing felt scary at first. It became one of her biggest strengths.
4. **Passion fuels perseverance.**
   When you care deeply, you don't quit—not even when people don't understand at first.
5. **Animals depend on us.**
   You can make a real difference in shelters, rescue groups, and your community.

Your Turn: Help an Animal Today

Just like Shelby, you can make life better for pets who need you.

If you visit a shelter, look for:

- animals who seem shy or overlooked
- darker-colored pets who don't get as many visitors
- cages people walk past without stopping
- posters or flyers asking for volunteers

Ask yourself:

"Who here needs a little extra attention?"

You might be the person who helps a quiet, waiting animal finally find their forever home.

CHAPTER 3

Using Math to Help a Community in Need

Gabrielle Tobin — Episode 77

A Birthday That Started a Movement

Gabrielle Tobin's Gold Award wasn't the start of her service—it was the continuation of something she began when she was only ten years old. On her 10th birthday, instead of asking for presents, Gabrielle donated school supplies to Lindley Sixth Grade Academy, a Title I school in Georgia. That single act of kindness grew into a long-term relationship with the school.

As she continued supporting Lindley Academy year after year, the staff and students took notice. By her third year of service, the school presented her with the Dr. Martin Luther King Jr. Humanitarian Award, an honor that surprised and humbled her. The award strengthened her resolve to continue supporting the school and to work closely with Principal Dr. Magee to address deeper educational needs.

Identifying the Problem: The Math Gap

When planning her Gold Award, Gabrielle knew she wanted her project to help Lindley Academy in a meaningful and sustainable way. Dr. Magee shared a major challenge: many of the school's sixth graders were struggling with math proficiency, and a large portion of the students were bilingual, speaking both English and Spanish.

Gabrielle realized that to make a lasting impact, her project needed to provide academic support that was accessible to every student. That's when she developed the idea that would become her Gold Award.

The Solution: For Math's Sake peer-to-peer videos

Gabrielle created a series of short, bilingual "peer-to-peer" math videos—videos where students teach other students. Her project resulted in:
- 13 bilingual videos
- Covered the entire sixth-grade math curriculum
- Short, clear, and easy to navigate
- Step-by-step demonstrations of essential math skills

To choose the exact topics, Gabrielle and Dr. Magee used the school's summer math packet. The goal was simple: make it easy for students to find *exactly* the help they needed, without sitting through long lessons.

Building the Team

A project this large required teamwork. Gabrielle recruited seven close friends to help film, edit, translate, and brainstorm creative ideas. She especially enjoyed the creative freedom of editing the videos and shaping them into helpful, engaging learning tools.

When the Pandemic Hit

The COVID-19 pandemic created unexpected challenges. Many schools were overwhelmed by the transition to remote learning, making it hard for Gabrielle to expand her project to other campuses.

Fortunately, her project was already digital. Students could watch the videos from home, making her work especially valuable during remote learning. The format allowed her project to continue when many others had to pause.

Personal Growth and Lasting Impact

Throughout the Gold Award process, Gabrielle strengthened her leadership skills and learned how to collaborate effectively with her team. She discovered the value of research—her mentor encouraged her to spend at least 2 weeks researching community needs, a step she credits with helping her design a meaningful, targeted project.
Before starting, she thought the Gold Award was "just a project I had to do." By the end, she realized it was an opportunity to make a real impact.

Media Spotlight

The success of "For Math's Sake" caught the attention of major news outlets. Gabrielle was interviewed by:
• NBC
• ABC
• Fox
• The Atlanta Journal-Constitution
• National Public Radio (NPR)
• Girl Scouts USA

She described the experience as "unexplainable and unimaginable," and she was grateful for the opportunity to share her project with a wider audience.

The Legacy Continues

Gabrielle's work eventually led her to create her own 501 (c) (3) nonprofit foundation, 40 Mustard Seeds, in honor of the school. Through the foundation, she continues to supply materials and support students in partnership with her former daycare.

Future Goals

Beyond her Gold Award, Gabrielle is an active and talented student. She has attended Camp CEO, served on the older girl advisory board, and earned both her Silver and Gold Awards. She is a dedicated gymnast and has played the cello for 7 years, finding classical music calming and stress-relieving.

Looking ahead, Gabrielle plans to attend college and pursue a career in the medical field. Her dream is to become an oncologist.

Chapter 4

Learning to Communicate with Working Dogs

Kaitlyn Maloney (Ep 53)

A Chance Encounter That Changed Everything

For Kaitlyn Maloney, her Gold Award journey began with a moment of pure curiosity—and four paws. At a local event called National Night Out, she noticed a table run by The Seeing Eye, an organization that trains guide dogs for people who are blind.

Her first thought was simple:
"I love dogs. I just want to play with dogs."

The volunteers shared something deeper. These weren't just puppies—they were future guide dogs with a life-changing job. Kaitlyn was struggling to come up with a Gold Award idea at the time, and suddenly it clicked. She wanted a project that wasn't too small, something big and meaningful. Raising a guide dog felt "a little big in the end," and important enough to take on.

After long conversations, her hesitant parents finally agreed, and Kaitlyn entered the world of professional puppy raising. She began with meetings, training practice, and babysitting another guide dog before receiving her own permanent puppy: Rosalie, a German Shepherd.

The Strict Rules of a Seeing Eye Dog

Raising a future guide dog was nothing like training a family pet. These dogs must stay calm, focused, and reliable in every situation—they guide people through crowded stores, busy sidewalks, airports, and traffic.

Kaitlyn quickly learned that the expectations were intense. She had to manage:

• **Vocalization:** Rosalie wasn't allowed to bark. But she *was* very vocal and would whine—a lot. Kaitlyn and her mom had to work

constantly to discourage it.
• **Jumping:** Rosalie loved to jump. Kaitlyn trained her to let no one pet her unless she was sitting.
• **Commands:** Rosalie learned "sit" on cue and mastered "park," a command meaning she had to use the bathroom right away.
• **Positioning:** Rosalie had to always stay on Kaitlyn's left side during walks.

But Kaitlyn didn't stop at training Rosalie. Her Gold Award centred on educating the public about what distracts guide dogs. She taught people:

• Don't call a guide dog's name.
• Don't talk to the dog.
• Don't pet the dog.
• Always speak to the handler, not the dog.
• If you have your own dog, move it away immediately.

To spread this message, Kaitlyn created flyers, a patch program called "Seeing Eye Girl," and a slideshow video documenting Rosalie's training. She explained the difference between general service dogs and seeing-eye dogs, which must know how to navigate roads, judge traffic, and notice dangers on their own.

Training in the Real World

The most exciting part of raising a guide dog was taking Rosalie into places pets usually aren't allowed. Kaitlyn trained her in:

• Grocery stores
• Local gyms
• Outdoor festivals
• Sit-down restaurants

The mall was Rosalie's favorite, though it was the hardest. So many people, smells, and distractions—it was a true test.

Kaitlyn practiced with Rosalie at the airport, rehearsing how to walk onto a plane and sit calmly in tight spaces. While they never left the ground, the training prepared Rosalie for the day she might fly with her future partner.

The Biggest Roadblocks

Kaitlyn started her Gold Award during her junior year, a time packed with AP and Honors courses, varsity sports (soccer and lacrosse), and SAT prep. She strongly advises younger Girl Scouts to start earlier if they can.

Her biggest challenge was one no one saw coming:

 COVID-19 Shut Down Everything

When the pandemic hit:

- All in-person training stopped.
- Rosalie couldn't go to stores or malls.
- She became an inside dog, losing motivation and practice.
- Kaitlyn struggled to stay motivated, too.

To keep going, she moved her patch program online to Zoom, where participants asked questions, shared progress, and tried to support one another. Even though everything was harder, Kaitlyn refused to quit. She reminded herself why she started—and kept showing up for Rosalie.

The Vest Test and Rosalie's Final Success

Kaitlyn's most stressful—and favorite—memory was Rosalie's vest test, which would determine if she was ready to wear the official guide dog vest.

It took place inside a Target. Rosalie smelled Kaitlyn's mom somewhere in the store and began whining loudly. For a moment, Kaitlyn feared the dog would fail.

But after patiently working with her, Rosalie settled, followed commands, and passed the test.

Then came the biggest news of all.

Instead of being matched with a blind handler, Rosalie was selected for The Seeing Eye's breeding program. This meant she had the best possible genetics and temperament—the kind of qualities the organization wanted to pass on to future guide dog puppies.

It was a moment of immense pride for Kaitlyn and her family.

Lessons That Shaped the Future

Kaitlyn learned major life skills during her Gold Award:

- prioritization
- organization
- communication
- perseverance through unexpected challenges

She remembered lessons from her Silver Award—where she and her troop taught table manners and food health—and used those organizational skills to lead her Gold Award alone.

Her advice to younger Girl Scouts:
Avoid procrastination, stay focused, and "always ask for help." Parents, troop leaders, teachers, and other Girl Scouts are there to support you.

Kaitlyn attends James Madison University, majoring in health sciences and planning a career in physical therapy. She plays club soccer and hopes to start a Seeing Eye club on campus, allowing Rosalie's legacy to continue inspiring others.

Chapter 5

Speaking Up to Keep Pets Safe

Annie Hsiao (Ep 160)

A Voice for the Voiceless

For Annie Hsiao, the idea for her Gold Award project, "South Florida Pet Safety," grew from her lifelong love of animals. Annie dreams of becoming a veterinarian and deeply believes in advocating for animals because they don't have a voice.

She began by identifying a startling problem: in her community, up to 30% of all pet deaths are preventable accidents—situations where pet owners didn't realize the dangers around them. Annie knew she needed to create an awareness campaign to teach people how to keep their pets safe, especially in South Florida's unique environment.

A Pet Safety Book Like No Other

You can find general pet safety tips online; however, South Florida has specific hazards that newcomers often aren't aware of. Because the region is a "transient community"—with many retirees, vacationers, and new residents—Annie realized an educational gap existed.

Her solution was to create a comprehensive, South-Florida-specific pet safety book with four major sections:

1. **Heat Dangers** — Warning about extreme temperatures and hot cars.
2. **Wildlife** — Explaining threats like alligators and other predators.
3. **Plants** — Identifying toxic or dangerous native plants.
4. **Natural Disasters** — Including hurricane prep and drowning prevention.

Much of her book was shaped by her past science fair work. For example, she knew how dangerous hot cars could be because she studied them. Another project focused on Bufo toads, an invasive species whose poison can kill pets, especially small dogs. Her research helped her teach pet owners how to prevent poisonings and what to do if it happens.

Raising Money and Spreading the Word

Gold Award rules require girls to figure out their funding independently. For Annie, this was one of the hardest parts—until she devised a clever sponsorship model.

If someone donated $25, they would:
• sponsor the printing of 10 books
• receive one book for free

The plan worked incredibly well. Although she originally planned to print 100 copies, her fundraising efforts were so successful that she ended up printing 500 copies—five times her initial goal.

The books were distributed at the Humane Society and given to families adopting pets. To keep the project going after the printed books were gone, Annie added QR codes at community locations that linked to a free digital PDF of her book.

Addressing the Vet Shortage

While working on her Gold Award, Annie discovered another issue: the national shortage of veterinarians. There are only 32 veterinary schools in the U.S., compared to nearly 200 medical schools, and the surge in pet ownership during the pandemic amplified the shortage.

Annie responded by starting a pre-vet club at her school to inspire more students to consider the field.

The club quickly became active and impactful:
• They brought in guest speakers—including vets from the Humane

Society clinic.
 • Annie hosted a renowned veterinary dentist, Dr. Bellows.
 • They held dog washes and raised money for animal disaster relief.

To ensure the club would outlive her graduation, she established a leadership chain, allowing new officers to take over each year and ensuring long-term sustainability.

Workshops and Social Media Outreach

Annie expanded her campaign through teaching and digital outreach.

Workshops:
She taught pet-safety sessions for Girl Scouts and incorporated her book into badge programs, including the Junior Animal Helper and Brownie Pets badges.

Lower School Education:
She partnered with her school's lower school principal to teach environmental education lessons to younger students. Their responses were heartfelt—one child wrote "best presentation ever" on a survey.

Social Media:
She created an Instagram account to post timely reminders—such as firework safety tips for the Fourth of July.

Community Partnerships:
Annie visited pet-friendly hotels and stores, such as Pet Supermarket, to ask if she could post flyers with the book's QR code. Many said yes simply because she asked.

Connections That Changed Her Future

Annie spent nearly 200 hours on her project. One of her biggest lessons was that people are often incredibly willing to help when you reach out—especially in the Girl Scout community.

Her project opened unexpected doors. Her expert advisor, Darlene Feldman, Director of Education at the Humane Society, helped Annie secure a position in the Humane Society surgical clinic. Although the role was typically for people 18 or older, Annie's dedication earned her the opportunity.

She gained hands-on experience by observing surgeries and preparing surgical packs—an opportunity she described as a "really cool experience." These experiences confirmed what she already knew: becoming a veterinarian is her true calling.

Her Gold Award taught her discipline, collaboration, and confidence, particularly through challenges such as launching the pre-vet club and writing the book. She now plans to major in biology or animal science in college, ready to pursue her dream.

Annie wants future Girl Scouts to know that while the Gold Award can be difficult, it is absolutely worth it. The skills, confidence, and impact will stay with you for the rest of your life.

CHAPTER 6
Saving a Shoreline from Erosion

Rachel Mazcyk (Ep 14)

A Shoreline in Trouble

When Rachel Mazyck walked along the edge of her Florida bay, she noticed something most people missed: The shoreline was shrinking.

Storms hit harder. The sandy banks looked thinner. Even the water seemed cloudier than usual.

Rachel loved this place. She explored it with friends, watched birds along the rocks, and knew every curve of the coastline. Seeing it slowly disappear didn't just bother her — it worried her.

She asked herself a question that changes everything:

"If I see a problem…, what can I do to fix it?"

The Hidden Enemy: Invasive Species

As Rachel researched the shoreline, she discovered two major problems:

1. Invasive plants

Plants that didn't belong there were spreading fast, crowding out the native ones that protected the soil.

Her observation? Imagine pythons in the Everglades — animals with no natural competition can take over quickly. The same thing was happening with certain plants along her bay.

2. Erosion from rising water

Waves were pulling soil away, and without strong roots, the land had nothing to hold it in place.

If nothing changed, the coastline could disappear completely —
along with the wildlife that depended on it.

Rachel didn't want that to happen. To solve the problem, she found
a solution hidden in nature itself.

Meet the Mangroves: Nature's Shoreline Superheroes

Mangroves are amazing trees with twisty roots that stretch into the
water like long fingers. They:

- protect the shores from storms
- trap soil and stop erosion
- give fish and crabs places to live
- filter pollution

But in Rachel's area, mangroves were losing the battle against
invasives.

She made a bold decision: She would grow new mangroves…
hundreds of them.

A Year of Growing Hope

Rachel's Gold Award project began with collecting mangrove seeds
— sometimes 300 to 400 in one trip. She took them to a
greenhouse at FIU's Biscayne Bay Campus and cared for them
every week.

This wasn't a quick project. It was a year-long commitment,
watering, checking, and tending each plant. If a sudden Florida
rainstorm rolled in, she sometimes had to sprint a full mile back to
the main building.

It was slow, steady, patient work. Even that wasn't the hardest part.

The Big "No"

For four months, Rachel tried to partner with her dream location, Pelican Bay Harbor.

Each time she asked, she received an answer like:

"We're under new management… maybe later."

Then one day, the answer became a clear, final:

"No."

She said it felt "like a slap in the face." After months of effort, research, and planning, the rejection stung.

But later, she realized something powerful: That "no" was her most important lesson.

It taught her that one rejection isn't the end. If you keep going, *there is always a yes somewhere.*

Clearing the Way

Mangroves may be strong protectors, but they're surprisingly weak competitors. They struggle against invasive plants.

To give her seedlings a real chance, Rachel and her team had to:

- dig up invasive plants
- remove full-grown saplings
- clear large areas by hand

It was sweaty, muddy, exhausting work. But every patch they cleared opened a space for new mangroves to thrive.

Planting a Future Shoreline

Once the land was ready, Rachel led volunteers in planting the mangrove seedlings she'd raised for a year.

She taught them why mangroves mattered.
She showed them where to plant each one.
Together, they created a living barrier that would help protect the coast long after their project ended.

Over the following months, the results became visible:

- The soil stayed in place.
- Water flowed more gently.
- Wildlife slowly returned.

Her project didn't just repair a problem — it transformed the shoreline.

The Toughest Battle: Her Own Doubt

Even with all the hard physical work, Rachel said her biggest obstacle wasn't weather, plants, or rejection.

It was herself.

She hesitated for five months before submitting her Gold Award proposal. Not because she didn't care — she feared failing.

She worried the council reviewing her proposal would judge her harshly. She worried her idea wasn't good enough. She worried she couldn't finish something that big.

But little by little, she realized something important:

The council wasn't her enemy — they wanted her to succeed. Their critiques are not to hurt you; they are intended to help you. They want the project to showcase your best potential.

Once she pushed past her fear, everything changed. She completed the project just one month before the deadline — proving to herself that she *could* do difficult, meaningful things.

Rachel's Biggest Takeaway

After two years of work, hundreds of seedlings, and countless obstacles, Rachel walked away with a belief that will shape the rest of her life:

"I can do anything."

She learned:

- patience
- endurance
- pride
- confidence

And she saw that her actions made a real difference for her community.

What You Can Learn from Rachel

1. **Start small — just notice things.** Big problems often begin with tiny changes.
2. **Don't let fear delay your ideas.** Rachel waited five months before taking the first step.

3. **Rejection isn't the end.** One "no" doesn't erase your "yes."
4. **Nature has powerful solutions.** The mangroves were the real heroes — Rachel only helped them return.
5. **You can help your community too.** You don't need to solve everything alone.

Your Turn: Become a Shoreline Superhero

Wherever you live — near a lake, river, wetland, or coast — look for:

- signs of erosion
- invasive plants
- changing water patterns
- places that could use some care

Then ask the same question that changed Rachel's life:

"What can *I* do to help?"

Small actions add up. And who knows? Your idea might save a shoreline too.

Chapter 7

Building Homes for Pollinators

Cerise Mensah (Ep 30)

A Passion for Protecting Wildlife

For Girl Scout Cerise Mensah, the path to her Gold Award began with a deep love for wildlife and a desire to protect it. She knew from the start that her project needed to focus on conservation. Finding the *right* project—one that was meaningful and realistic—took time and reflection.

Like many Girl Scouts, Cerise started with a bold idea. She wanted to make a big difference. But learning when to pivot turned out to be one of her most important leadership lessons.

The Problem of the Pivot

Cerise's first idea was ambitious: a "roadkill app" designed to track and organize the cleanup of roadkill along highways and roads. While creative and well-intentioned, the reality quickly became clear. App development, coordination, and large-scale logistics would take far more time than a high school Gold Award allowed.

Cerise and her mom realized it would be a "very, very tedious and long process"—one that simply wasn't attainable at that stage of her life.

Cerise did something smart.
She pivoted.

Instead of abandoning conservation altogether, she chose a project that was focused, sustainable, and achievable: building a bee hotel for native pollinators at the Chattahoochee Nature Preserve in Georgia.

Architecture Meets Ecology

The bee hotel was far more than a simple box. It required Cerise to combine hands-on construction with ecological research.

She began with the structure itself, finding a second-hand wooden chest from a thrift store. To prepare it for outdoor use, she sanded it down, removed the exterior finish, and applied a protective coating to help it withstand Georgia's harsh weather.

The real challenge was designing the inside.

Cerise quickly learned that conservation conversations often focus only on honeybees. Pollination depends on many species, including butterflies and hummingbirds. She asked herself a simple question: "Bee hotel sounds cool… what does that actually mean?"

Through research, she discovered she could support at least seven different native pollinators by creating specialized compartments inside the chest.

She designed the interior with intention:
• Wood blocks for carpenter bees, which naturally drill into wood.
• Bedding and leaves to attract other native bee species.
• Other natural materials suited to different pollinator needs.

She learned an important logistical lesson. Filling the compartments at home would have made transporting the hotel a disaster. Instead, she waited and completed the final setup on-site at the Nature Preserve, avoiding what she joked would have been "a catastrophe" involving her dad's truck.

Research, Partnership, and Support

Cerise's partnership with the Chattahoochee Nature Preserve made her project stronger from the start. The Preserve listed a bee hotel as a possible project on its website, making the initial connection easy.

She worked closely with an advisor from the Preserve, who understood the local ecosystem and guided her research. Cerise stayed in regular contact with him because he knew not only about pollinators and what the Preserve specifically needed, but also about the Preserve itself.

This collaboration ensured the bee hotel wasn't generic—it was tailored to the environment it served.

Time Management and Trusting Support

Cerise openly admits her biggest personal challenge was time management. She described herself as a "huge procrastinator," and her project timeline overlapped with senior year, graduation activities, classes, and playing soccer.

Her greatest support came from her mom.
She credits her mom with keeping the project on track—reminding her what needed to be done, helping her plan next steps, and driving her wherever she needed to go.

Cerise is honest about it: without that support, she doesn't believe she would have finished the project. Through this experience, she learned that leadership doesn't mean doing everything alone—it means accepting help.

A New Path and a Lasting Legacy

Cerise's favorite moment came at the final installation of the bee hotel at the Nature Preserve. Her troop and family showed up to support her, and seeing everyone there made the long process feel worth it.

More importantly, the project changed her future.

Before her Gold Award, Cerise thought she wanted to become a veterinarian. But through her research, she realized there was much more to helping animals than clinical care. Conservation biology opened her eyes to a new path—one focused on ecosystems, habitats, and long-term impact.

She is now studying wildlife conservation and conservation biology, confident that this is work she truly loves.

Her advice to future Girl Scouts is simple and sincere:
The work is hard, and if you're passionate about your project, it's deeply rewarding.

Cerise's bee hotel stands as proof that when conservation is built with curiosity, persistence, and heart, it can change both an ecosystem and a life.

Chapter 8

Saving Water and Protecting Our World

Isabela Santiago Reyes (Ep 136)

Understanding the Power of Water

Isabela Santiago Reyes knew exactly what she wanted to focus on for her Gold Award: water. Living near Girl Scout Camp Dorothy Thomas (CDT), she realized that even people who loved the outdoors didn't always understand how their daily habits affected the planet. For Isabela, the challenge wasn't just fixing things—it was teaching people why water efficiency matters. When people understand *why* something is important, they are far more likely to protect it.

Her project began with two practical improvements at CDT, which became the foundation for her larger mission:
• She replaced the camp's old showerheads with new, water-efficient models, saving water with every shower.
• She installed two large rain barrels, which collect rainwater that can later be used for plants and outdoor needs.

To ensure her work continued long after she finished, she added signs around the camp explaining water-conservation practices.

Once the physical improvements were complete, Isabela shifted to community education. She met with Girl Scout troops in person and over Zoom, teaching groups ranging from eight girls to as many as twenty-five.

The Test of Public Speaking

The biggest challenge came when Isabela set up an information booth at a local Lowe's store to reach the public. Her mission was to teach shoppers how to conserve water, what to look for in efficient products, and which government rebates were available for water-saving devices sold right in the store.

But there was a problem: Isabela hated public speaking.

Asking strangers, "Hi! Would you like to learn about water conservation?" felt terrifying. Many shoppers brushed past her, assuming she was selling something or asking for donations. Lowe's customers usually shop with a purpose, not everyone had time to stop.

Isabela felt discouraged, and she refused to quit. She reminded herself to roll with the punches—not everyone will stop to talk, and that's okay. She kept going, and over one weekend, she spoke to at least 100 people, a huge accomplishment for someone afraid of public speaking.

Her biggest lesson from the booth was simple and powerful: "Don't be afraid." Most people were friendly once she got a chance to speak, and facing her fears showed her she was stronger than she realized.

Building a Team and Accepting Help

Although a single Girl Scout leads the Gold Award, it is far too big to do alone. Isabela learned this quickly as she balanced her team, her planning, and the lengthy approval process.

One of her biggest hurdles was the amount of paperwork required. She spent hours writing her final report, trimming sections to fit the strict character counts on the website. Her advice for future Gold Award Girl Scouts is clear: write everything in Google Docs first. Then you can track your word count and avoid losing work.

Isabela struggled at first with accepting help. She believed the Gold Award had to be completely her work. She soon realized that strong leadership means allowing others to support you. Her team included:
• Ranger Steve, the camp ranger, who helped with guidance and ideas.
• A University of Florida advisor, whom she met during a class on water barrels, and who provided technical expertise on micro-irrigation and conservation.
• Her troop members, who helped install signs around the camp.

When she led large troop meetings with up to twenty-five girls, she asked her friends to help manage the groups. This delegation made the sessions run smoothly and allowed her to focus on teaching.

A New Chapter: The Global Adventure

After overcoming her fears, leading a team, and educating her community, Isabela was ready for the next challenge—*the world*.

She applied for and was accepted into a Girl Scout Destination trip to Sangam, the World Association of Girl Guides and Girl Scouts (WAGGGS) World Center in Pune, India. It was her first time leaving the country without her parents.

She joined girls from across the United States, as well as participants from Japan, on a 14-hour flight. Many of them were nervous; they had heard scary stories about diseases or human trafficking. Sharing their worries made them feel less alone.

At Sangam, Isabela learned that India has the largest number of Girl Guides in the world, and that in many places, guiding is linked directly to schooling. She noticed that the uniforms were different too—some girls wore crisp white shirts, ties, and hats.

Her trip included meaningful service work. She visited local homes for people with physical and intellectual disabilities, helped with activities, and learned from the staff. The leaders at Sangam kept the group safe, choosing restaurants with filtered water and guiding them through markets.

The experience of traveling with girls from around the world, exploring a new culture, and serving others convinced Isabela that the world was bigger—and more connected—than she ever imagined. While the United States is huge, she realized that traveling internationally opens an entire world of learning and perspective.

What Isabela Learned

Her Gold Award taught her lessons she will take into every part of her future:
• Be passionate about your project.
• Stick with your goals, even when things get hard.
• Don't try to do everything alone—leadership includes accepting help.
• Facing fears (like public speaking) builds confidence that lasts a lifetime.

Isabela's journey—from fixing showerheads to conquering international travel—shows how one Girl Scout can create real change at home and discover a bigger world at the same time.

Chapter 9

Cooling Down a Community the Smart Way

Montserrat Hidalgo (Ep 152)

Growing Up in a Hot Spot

Montserrat Hidalgo grew up in Southgate, a city in Southeast Los Angeles, where she noticed something unfair: her community faced environmental problems that wealthier neighborhoods didn't. Factories sat too close to schools, soil was contaminated with lead, and the air was filled with toxins linked to asthma and cancer.

This wasn't just something she saw on the news—it affected her own family. Montserrat had asthma, and her sister struggled with lung issues. When she started learning more environmental science, she realized these health problems were rooted in environmental racism, a pattern where communities of color often live in more polluted areas.

"You don't know that you deserve clean air, clean water, clean soil until you go out and learn about it," she said. And once she learned the truth, she couldn't ignore it.

Mapping the Problem

To better understand the issue, Montserrat joined a high-level research project through NASA, Chapman University, and UC Irvine. Using QGIS (mapping software) and ECO Stress (a NASA satellite that measures surface temperature), she analyzed how heat affected different neighborhoods.

The results shocked her.

Her community was significantly hotter than nearby, primarily white, and more affluent areas. The concrete, blacktop, and lack of trees created an "urban heat island," trapping heat and making daily life more dangerous.

This discovery gave her a clear mission:
Lower the surface temperatures in her neighborhood.

A Stolen Idea and a Test of Grit

Montserrat's first plan was to cool down her high school's large black asphalt blacktop, a surface that often reached 120–130°F in the California heat. She found the right kind of reflective paint, secured district approval, and was ready to start.

But then things fell apart.

The company she was working with suddenly stopped responding. When she rewrote her proposal and resubmitted it, the district denied it.

The reason was heartbreaking:
The superintendent stole her idea and implemented it himself.

Shortly after, the city mayor, who coached at the high school, tried to take credit for proposing something similar.

Montserrat felt crushed.
She said she felt powerless—just a young woman of color watching adult men take her work and erase her voice.

"It was really saddening… I was ready to give up on my project at that point."

She only continued because of the support of her mother, her troop leaders, and her fellow Gold Award Girl Scouts who were fighting their own battles.

Her resilience through what her council called an insane number of hardships later helped her earn the GSUSA National Gold Award Scholarship.

The Solution: Paint, Plants, and People Power

After the school shut her out, Montserrat shifted her project to the city level. She partnered with the Southgate Parks and Recreation Department and brought her vision to life at Hollydale Park.

Her strategy relied on a simple scientific fact:
Dark colors absorb heat; light colors reflect it.

She led volunteers in a two-part solution:

1. **Painting the Pavement:** They covered areas of pavement with lighter, heat-reflective paint.

2. **Planting Native Species:** They planted 40 California native plants, which naturally cool the environment and support local ecosystems.

Volunteers included members of the Youth Action environmental justice club she founded at her high school. Experts came to teach proper planting techniques, turning the event into a hands-on community learning experience.

The results were measurable and impressive.
Surface temperatures dropped from 98°F to about 89°F, including during cooler winter months. A 12-degree reduction proved that her combination of reflective paint and native plants worked.

A Legacy of Science and Advocacy

Montserrat's Gold Award became a model for community-driven environmental justice. She partnered with organizations such as Communities for a Better Environment and Tree People, which supported her event and helped spread awareness.

Her experiences—both the victories and the injustices—solidified her career path. Today, she studies at Williams College and plans to double major in environmental studies and biology. Her goal is to earn a Ph.D. and use science to support policy changes in environmental justice communities.

Montserrat's story shows that real change often begins with the people most affected by a problem—and that science, community, and courage can reshape a neighborhood.

Her work cools more than pavement.
It cools the conversation, quiets injustice, and sparks hope.

Montserrat's project is like a powerful air conditioner for her community—proving that with science, determination, and heart, the hottest, most overlooked places can find relief.

Chapter 10

Standing Up Against Plastic Pollution

Shelby O'Neil (Ep 46)

Falling in Love with the Ocean

Shelby O'Neil didn't grow up by the ocean. She lived 45 minutes inland in California, where dirt and parks felt more familiar than waves. But everything changed when she joined the Young Women in Science program at the Monterey Bay Aquarium. There, she saw the ocean's beauty, mystery, and limitlessness, and she was stunned.

That moment transformed Shelby from a girl who barely thought about the ocean into a girl who wanted to protect it.

She began asking a big question: How can ordinary people have a personal, meaningful impact on the environment?

Her answer eventually became a nonprofit—Junior Ocean Guardians—and a global movement known as No Straw November.

The Gateway Problem: Plastic Straws

When Shelby first began speaking out against plastic straws, almost no one understood why they mattered. Straws were viewed as harmless conveniences, not environmental hazards.

But Shelby saw their potential: Plastic straws are the perfect "gateway" to environmental awareness.

For most people who don't medically need straws, giving them up is:
• easy
• immediate
• meaningful

She taught that straws are *not recyclable* and often end up in the ocean, harming marine life. Eliminating one straw could open the door to larger changes—like reducing all single-use plastics.

But education alone wasn't enough. Shelby wanted corporate change.

She did something bold: She emailed CEOs of major corporations, asking them to eliminate plastic straws.

This took enormous resilience. Many ignored her. Some pushed back.
But Shelby persisted—relentlessly.

Her efforts led to major victories:
• Alaska Airlines cut millions of straws from in-flight service.
• Dignity Health removed plastic straws from cafeterias and educated their staff.
• Costco engaged with her proposals.

One unforgettable moment was meeting with Starbucks at their enormous Seattle campus. High-school Shelby felt like she was "internally dying" from excitement. She talked through the pros and cons of "sippy cup lids," discussed flaws in recycling, and learned that Starbucks had a beekeeping club on its roof.

Her biggest networking tip?
Google the CEO and reach out through LinkedIn.
You have more access than you think.

From Classroom Challenge to National Law

No Straw November began in a classroom. Shelby noticed that students knew plastic pollution was harmful. She didn't know what to *do* about it. She needed a simple, actionable challenge that helped kids reflect on their habits.

The name came to her naturally, and almost instantly she saw its power.

Every year, the challenge partners with groups like youth artists and organizations focused on voting rights. But the movement didn't stop in classrooms.

Shelby founded Junior Ocean Guardians to support her educational outreach, which led her into the world of policy and legislation.

She became a key witness for California's AB184, the bill requiring restaurants to provide single-use plastic straws only upon request.

Shelby was strategic.
She explained to lawmakers that the policy was not only environmentally smart—it was economically beneficial. Restaurants would save money by not automatically giving away straws that people didn't need.

She learned how the movement of a resolution through the Senate helped build political support for AB184.

Her advocacy skills—and her courage—helped shape a piece of state law.

Becoming a Relentless Communicator

Shelby's Gold Award changed her more than she expected.
She discovered she loved communication—not just speaking but uplifting scientists and sharing environmental truths with the world.

But mastering communication wasn't the only challenge.

Starting her nonprofit was expensive. To fund it, she took her first job at Gilroy Gardens, an amusement park, where she learned the importance of financial responsibility and saving.

She faced another critical lesson: Not everyone will agree with you—even when the science is clear.

Her solution was simple and powerful: Be relentless.

She joked that she became like the Lorax—speaking for the environment when people didn't want to listen. And she stressed that everyone, including those who live far from the coast, affects the ocean and is affected by it.

Full Circle Moments and a Lasting Legacy

Shelby's work earned her national recognition as one of the 10 National Gold Award Girl Scouts for 2018. It was a whirlwind—two trips to New York in one week, media attention, and new opportunities to inspire younger girls.

One of the most surprising moments? Sesame Street. Shelby cold-emailed the CEO, asking how they planned to teach kids about the environment. Eventually, she was invited to their headquarters and filmed a segment—an experience she calls one of her all-time favorites.

But her most meaningful memory was small and heartfelt.

After teaching a class in her hometown, she handed out No Straw November activity books and patches. A little girl ran full speed out of the room to show her family what she had earned. Seeing that joy, Shelby thought:

"That's why I'm doing this."

Her legacy continues through her nonprofit, her movement, and her academic path. Shelby chose to major in society and environment at UC Berkeley, focusing on global environmental politics. Her Gold Award sparked a lifelong career of advocacy and leadership.

Chapter 11

Planting Trees to Shape the Future

Anita Werderich (Ep 162)

Asking the Right Question

For Anita Werderich, the journey to her Girl Scout Gold Award didn't begin with a giant idea. It started with a simple, thoughtful question: "What does my hometown need?"

Growing up in Yorkville, Illinois, she realized that her town's beloved riverfront had a hidden problem: low biodiversity. The river's constant flow eroded the soil, making it difficult for trees to survive when water levels changed. The issue wasn't just environmental—it affected the beauty and long-term stability of a place where her community gathered.

Anita knew her project needed to help the riverfront thrive again. She set out to plant strong, native Illinois trees that could withstand fluctuating water levels and increase biodiversity. Her goal: protect the land, strengthen the ecosystem, and give her community a healthier, more beautiful outdoor space.

Starting with a Conversation

Instead of guessing what to do, Anita went straight to the experts: the Yorkville Parks and Recreation Department. She asked them directly,
"What needs to be built on in this town? What do I need to do to make this city better?"

They loved her determination and pointed her toward tree planting along the riverfront. Anita immediately "dove right into it," beginning with research.

She learned that planting only one type of tree would be risky—an insect infestation could wipe out the entire area. What the riverfront needed was diverse, native species.

Her project advisor, Scott Slezer, guided her through the science of choosing species that could handle wet soil, flooding, and shifting river levels. With his help, she selected five native Illinois tree species and mapped the exact locations for all 20 trees.

Building the Green Team

Planting 20 trees takes a village. Anita recruited volunteers from every part of her life:
• classmates
• dance team
• cross country teammates
• National Honor Society members

She found that spreading the word and asking for help were essential skills. And after the planting was done, she invited younger Girl Scouts to help water the trees. This not only supported the project's long-term success but also allowed her to mentor younger girls—something she found deeply meaningful.

The Struggle for Communication

The fun part was planting. The difficult part? City communication.

People working in Parks and Recreation—and city government in general—were incredibly busy. Emails went unanswered. Meetings were delayed. Plans took longer than expected. Anita called this challenge a major "roadblock" because, at times, it felt like her project would never move forward.

To keep going, she had to build one of the most important life skills of all:
proactive communication.

She learned she couldn't wait around. She needed to follow up, send reminders, double-check permissions, and keep the project moving.

Her dad taught her the mantra she repeated throughout the project: "If you need something done, if you have a question—just ask."

That mindset became her superpower.

Balancing Sports and Service

As a three-sport athlete—cross country, dance, and track—Anita already had a packed schedule. Doing her Gold Award during junior and senior year meant her days often looked like this:

School → sports practice → Gold Award work → repeat.

She constantly communicated with her coaches, fit meetings into small pockets of time, and learned how to prioritize. Waiting for the right weather added another layer of challenge. Since she began the project in December, she had to time the planting carefully, so it wasn't too cold, too hot, too dry, or too rainy. Weather delays made the project feel endless at times.

But these challenges helped her develop strong time management skills—skills she knew would help her long after graduation.

The Lesson of Teaching

When the 20 trees were planted and the project was officially complete, Anita realized she had learned something unexpected: She loved teaching.

Helping younger Girl Scouts and explaining her environmental project sparked something new in her. She discovered that her passion wasn't just for nature. She wanted to help others understand it.

This realization shaped her future.

Anita studies mathematics for secondary education at the University of Illinois Chicago, where she is a member of the cross-country and track teams. She credits her Gold Award for helping her find her path.

Her dedication was recognized when she was named the GSUSA scholarship winner for her council, a moment she called her "last hurrah" as a Girl Scout.

Looking back, Anita encourages younger girls to stay in Girl Scouts, especially when the journey gets long or challenging. She believes the organization provides incredible opportunities and helps girls discover their strengths.

Her message is simple and powerful: Make the most of every experience and blossom into the beautiful person you are meant to be.

Chapter 12

Turning Waste Into Wealth

Katie Kahn (Ep 78)

A Legacy of Discovery

Katie Kahn was never one to settle for just the basics. While many students see science as a set of facts in a heavy textbook, Katie saw it as a toolkit for changing the world. Long before she began her most ambitious final project for the program, she had already dedicated years to exploring how the natural world worked. For over a decade, she had been part of a movement of girls committed to leadership and service, starting way back in kindergarten. By the time she reached high school, she had already earned two significant leadership awards, both rooted in science. This wasn't a coincidence; Katie felt a deep, personal pull toward the environment, a passion that only grew as she got older.

The real "lightbulb moment" for her project happened in a place where many great ideas are born: the classroom. During her sophomore and junior years of high school, Katie found herself sitting in an Advanced Placement (AP) Environmental Science class taught by Dr. Gerald Pollock. Dr. Pollock wasn't just any teacher; he held a PhD in geology and had a way of making the earth's systems feel alive and urgent. As they discussed the cycles of nature, Katie realized that while her community was great at recycling plastic and glass, they were missing a huge piece of the puzzle: composting.

"I started my project around my sophomore/junior year of high school," Katie remembered. She noticed that even though people wanted to be green, they often felt that composting was too difficult, too smelly, or required too much space. She decided that her mission would be to simplify the process. She wanted to prove that anyone, regardless of where they lived, could turn their kitchen scraps into nutrient-rich soil. With Dr. Pollock as her advisor, she began designing a blueprint to take composting out of the "too hard" category and put it right into her neighbors' hands. She knew that to make a lasting impact, she had to move beyond the classroom and into the backyards and community centers of her town.

The Blueprint For The Bin

Designing a solution to a community-wide problem requires more than just a good idea; it requires a practical plan that people can follow. Katie realized that if she asked people to buy expensive, high-tech composting equipment, they probably wouldn't. Instead, she looked around for items people already had at home. She envisioned a system in which old laundry baskets, blanket storage containers, or even simple plastic bins from a local store could be transformed into "magic boxes" that turn trash into treasure. This was the core of her project: taking something recycled and using it to recycle even more.

Katie didn't just want to tell people what to do; she wanted to show them. She spent months researching the "science of the pile," learning exactly how to balance the elements of nature to avoid common composting pitfalls, like bad smells or attracting unwanted pests. She learned that a successful compost bin needs a specific recipe of "browns" and "greens." The "browns" provide carbon, and the "greens" provide nitrogen; when you mix them with a bit of water and air, the microbes go to work.

The project was carried out through a series of hands-on workshops, during which Katie acted as both a teacher and a coach. She visited summer camps, spoke to younger girls' troops, and even led sessions in school classrooms. To ensure the knowledge lasted long after her workshops ended, she developed a series of materials to guide her community:

A Seven-Step Guide: This pamphlet broke down the entire process from gathering bins to the final soil harvest.

A Technical YouTube Video: Katie filmed a detailed tutorial where she walked viewers through the drilling and layering process.

The "No-Go" List: She created clear signage stating that items like meat and dairy should never be placed in the bin to keep the system healthy and safe.

Community Partnerships: She worked with logistics experts and local photographers to document the project and spread the word via social media.

One of the most important parts of her workshops was the "hands-on" element. Katie would bring drills and show kids how to safely put holes in the bottom of their bins for drainage and air. She watched as they carefully layered soil, sticks, leaves, and banana peels. By the time they were done, the participants didn't just have a bin; they had the confidence to manage a biological system right in their own homes.

The Hectic Season

Even with a brilliant plan and a supportive team, life has a way of throwing a lot at a girl all at once. For Katie, the implementation phase of her project hit right during one of the most stressful times in a teenager's life: college application season. She found herself trying to manage a team of volunteers, host workshops, and film educational content while simultaneously writing essays and filling out forms for her future. The time management required was unlike anything she had ever experienced. "The time management between trying to get all of those in and trying to submit all of my final paperwork... was definitely one of the hardest parts," she admitted.

But the pressure didn't stop there. While she was finishing up her final project, Katie was also preparing for a major spiritual and personal milestone—her Bat Mitzvah. Her schedule became a whirlwind of activity. One hour, she would meet with her project team to discuss logistics and social media outreach; an hour later, she would sit with her Hebrew tutor, practicing for her ceremony. As the dates for both her project deadline and her Bat Mitzvah drew closer, her life became a masterclass in prioritization. She was sending project reports to the council committee, sending invitations for her celebration, and searching for a dinner venue.

To make matters even more complicated, Katie was navigating all of this during the height of the global pandemic. "It was a very rocky project experience... a super hectic time with COVID," she recalled. Many of her initial plans for large, in-person gatherings had to be reworked or delayed. She had to learn how to be patient, both with herself and with the world around her. She realized that a leader isn't someone who never faces obstacles, but someone who knows how to take a breath, look at the rubric, and tackle things one step at a time. Through the chaos, she kept her phone calendar updated with reminders, separating her school life, her religious life, and her service life into distinct blocks of time. This organization was her anchor in the storm, allowing her to reach the finish line of her project just as she was stepping into her future.

Dirt, Smiles, and Peer Pressure

One of the biggest internal challenges Katie faced was surprising: her own expectations. Having been a camp counselor for years, she went into the project thinking that teaching would be the easiest part. "I had always been a camp counselor, and so I was like, 'Oh, like kids are easy. This is going to be simple, " she laughed. However, she quickly discovered that while little kids might be eager to jump into a pile of dirt, people her own age were a different story. It was much harder to make her peers care about composting, something they might initially see as "uncool" or "gross."

This taught Katie a vital lesson about leadership and communication. She realized she couldn't use the same approach for everyone. When talking to younger children, she used simple terms like "browns and greens." When speaking to older groups or school officials, she pivoted to more scientific language, discussing nitrates and carbon cycles. She had to learn the "patience to sit down and say, 'What can I do differently? How can I adjust my material? " This flexibility helped her break through the stigma of 'smelly trash' and show her friends that environmental engineering was quite sophisticated.

Despite the challenges of peer recruitment, some of Katie's favorite memories came from the pure joy of the younger participants. She vividly remembers an event at a nearby neighborhood swim team where a little girl approached her with a bin, wanting to participate but feeling a bit hesitant about the mess. The girl looked at the bin and then at her own clean hands and told Katie, "I don't want to get my hands dirty. Like, could you help me mix this?" Katie didn't hesitate; she grabbed a shovel and began mixing the soil and organic waste while the little girl stood by, clapping and cheering with pure excitement. Someone captured a photo of that moment—Katie with a shovel, the girl with a huge smile—and it became the symbol of her project's success. It wasn't just about the compost; it was about the connection and the ability to inspire someone else to be excited about the earth, even if they weren't quite ready to get their hands in the mud yet.

The Harvest Of Leadership

As Katie reached the end of her project, she realized she had grown far more than the plants in her compost-enriched soil. She had transformed from a student who liked science into a leader who could manage a complex team, navigate a global pandemic, and successfully communicate with everyone from PhD geologists to hesitant elementary students. The impact of her work was visible across her community, as more families began using their "magic bins" to reduce waste and improve their gardens. But the impact on Katie's own future was perhaps the most significant result of all.

The project opened doors she hadn't even realized were there. When it came time to apply for college scholarships, Katie didn't just mention her project as a hobby; she used it as the centerpiece of her applications. "Use your project for any and every scholarship you can think of," she advised. "I must have applied to 10 scholarships just because of my project." Her dedication paid off, helping her secure a spot at the University of Georgia (UGA), where she is now a student in the College of Engineering. She is currently pursuing a degree in environmental engineering with a minor in geology.

Looking toward the future, Katie has her sights set on helping large-scale mining companies become more sustainable and environmentally responsible. Her advice to other girls who feel bogged down by the "tedious" paperwork or the "rocky" moments of a big project is simple: "Just don't give up. It is an amazing project. It will teach you so much about yourself and about communication and networking skills." Katie's story is a reminder that when you put in the hard work and stay true to the rubric of your dreams, you can turn a pile of scraps into a foundation for a lifelong career.

In the end, Katie learned that leadership is a lot like composting; you have to take the messy, "green" energy of a new idea and mix it with the sturdy, "brown" structure of a solid plan. It requires a bit of water, a lot of air, and a great deal of patience while things break down and rebuild. If you're willing to wait for the cycle to complete, you won't just end up with a finished project—you'll end up with the rich, fertile ground from which the rest of your life will grow.

CHAPTER 13

Your Planet Protector Toolkit

🌏 Every Big Change Starts with One Small Choice

After reading the stories in this book, you've met girls who planted forests, protected endangered animals, built homes for pollinators, cooled down city streets, restored coastlines, and fought for cleaner, safer communities. Their projects might seem huge — and they are. Here's the real secret: 🌱 Every big project started with one small choice. One moment of curiosity. One "What if we tried this…?" One girl deciding her voice matters. You have that power too. This final chapter is your Planet Protector Toolkit — a collection of tips, habits, and ideas inspired by the Earth Guardians in these pages. Use them to begin your own journey.

🐾 1. Start by Noticing

Earth Guardians don't walk past problems; they *see* them. Try this:

- Look around your neighbourhood, school, or park.
- What feels unhealthy, unsafe, or unbalanced?
- What animals or plants seem stressed?
- Where do people need help?

Ask yourself: "What seems small and really matters?" That's where most great projects begin.

2. Learn Before You Act

Every girl in this book did research before jumping in. You can too.

Use:

- library books
- science websites
- local nature centers
- environmental groups
- conversations with adults who understand the issue

Learning first helps you make smart choices and
avoid causing accidental harm.

For example:

- Want to plant new trees? Make sure they're native.
- Want to help stray animals? Connect with a shelter first.
- Want to restore a habitat? Learn which plants belong there.

Knowledge is your strongest tool.

3. Build a Support Team

No Earth Guardian works alone, and you don't have to either. Ask:

- classmates
- friends
- siblings
- teachers
- troop members
- community leaders

Even one teammate makes a difference.
Here's something the girls in this book learned:
Adults love helping young leaders.
Don't be afraid to ask.

🌿 4. Start Small, But Stay Consistent

Many projects begin with one simple action:

- one animal adopted
- one patch of invasive species was removed
- one native plant added
- one classroom lesson taught
- one community event organized

Small steps stack up quickly.
Choose something you can do this week.
Then something next month.
Then something next season.
Consistency makes you unstoppable.

✏️ 5. Make a Plan You Can Actually Use

A real plan doesn't need to be fancy. It just needs to be clear. Try writing:

- your goal
- your timeline
- the supplies you need
- the people who can support you
- what success will look like

Remember:
A plan is a map, not a prison.
You're allowed to adjust as you go.
The girls in this book did — and it only made their projects stronger.

🐝 6. Protect the Creatures Others Forget

Some animals don't feel famous or glamorous. But every species matters. You can:

- plant flowers for bees
- build shelters for outdoor cats (with guidance)
- keep pets safe from environmental hazards
- help adoptable animals find homes
- teach others how to behave around service dogs

When you help the smallest creatures, you strengthen the entire ecosystem.

💧 7. Be a Water, Energy, and Waste Detective

Your everyday habits matter. You can:

- shorten showers
- turn off the lights
- avoid single-use plastics
- recycle correctly
- bring a reusable bottle
- use cold water when possible
- fix dripping faucets

> You don't need a huge project to make a real impact.
> Your choices ripple outward — just like water.

🌍 8. Speak Up for the Planet

You have a voice. Use it. You can:

- give presentations
- make posters
- write letters to leaders
- teach younger students
- make videos or slideshows

- start a club
- write an article for your school paper

When you share what you care about, people listen.
When people listen, things change.

9. Celebrate Every Win (Even the Tiny Ones)

Earth Guardians don't wait for giant victories. They celebrate:

- every plant that grows
- every animal helped
- every piece of trash picked up
- every person inspired
- every step forward

You're not just completing a project.
You're becoming the kind of person who pays attention,
takes action, and cares deeply.
That's worth celebrating.

10. Your Journey Starts Now

You may not restore an entire shoreline.
You may not cool down an entire city.
You may not plant a whole forest.
You **can** start something today — right now — that grows into something big.

Because the truth is:
Earth Guardians aren't chosen. They're made.
One small decision at a time.
One caring person at a time.
One project, one plant, one voice at a time.

The next Earth Guardian?

 It's you.

ABOUT THE AUTHOR

Sheryl M. Robinson is a podcaster, mentor, and speaker dedicated to helping teens and young adults discover their unique gifts, talents, and abilities, creating a path toward their dreams.

Sheryl holds a Master of Arts in Servant Leadership from Viterbo University and a Bachelor's in Accounting from Southern Illinois University – Carbondale. She has been a proud member of Girl Scouts for more than 30 years. Her passion for supporting teens — especially those pursuing the Girl Scout Gold Award — led her to create *Hearts of Gold*, a YouTube series and podcast featuring Gold Award Girl Scouts from across the world.

In recognition of her work elevating and supporting the Girl Scout Highest Awards, Sheryl has been honored with the GSUSA Thanks II Award, the organization's highest recognition for service.

Recognizing the need for younger Girl Scouts to have resources and role models as they pursue the Bronze Award and Silver Award, Sheryl created this middle-grade book series to share inspiring stories of leadership, courage, and community change.

She deeply believes that the Girl Scout Highest Awards not only make the world a better place but also transform the Girl Scouts who earn them — building lifelong changemakers, confident problem-solvers, and compassionate leaders.

ACKNOWLEDGMENTS

Creating this book has been a journey shaped by many remarkable people, and I am deeply grateful for each of you.

To **my mom, Jean**, who first started me in Girl Scouts many years ago and planted the seeds of everything that would follow.

To **my daughter, Nikki**, a Bronze, Silver, and Gold Award Girl Scout whose dedication inspires me every day. Watching you flourish through each phase of your life is one of my greatest joys.

To **my husband, Mark,** thank you for always supporting me and the many plates you quietly set beside me while I typed away. I thank God for bringing you into my life every day.

To **Kenzie, Jamie, and Lydia,** thank you for reading the first draft and sharing thoughtful feedback. Your insights helped shape this book and made it stronger.

To **all the Gold Award Girl Scouts** who have shared their stories on the Hearts of Gold podcast — thank you for trusting me with your journeys. Your courage, creativity, and leadership inspire thousands.

To the **Girl Scout leaders, volunteers, and parents** who support these incredible young women: your encouragement makes meaningful change possible.

To **Cassie**, who encouraged me to restart my Girl Scout journey when my daughter joined Girl Scouts.

A heartfelt thank you to **Stacie and Shannan**, who have listened to me talk about this book for years and never stopped encouraging me to make it happen.

To **Walter**, my podcast editor for the first nine years, and **Tommy**, my new editor — and to their entire family, especially **Greg**, whose podcasting challenge a decade ago helped set all of this into motion.

And finally, to **Elsie, Rob, Cliff, Daniel, and Jessica** — thank you for your inspiration, for keeping the process fun, for sharing your knowledge, and for helping Hearts of Gold continue to grow.

This project exists because of each of you.
Thank you for helping bring these stories to life.

To all the future Bronze, Silver, and Gold Award Girl Scouts and others inspired by this book – Be the change you want to see in the world and remember <u>your</u> leadership matters.

MORE STORIES

Want more inspiring stories from Gold Award Girl Scouts?

You can watch or listen to new episodes every month.

Podcast:
https://bit.ly/3JT7x0w

YouTube:
https://bit.ly/3P5nns8

Instagram:
https://bit.ly/3JZ2JX8

www.ingramcontent.com/pod-product-compliance
Lightning Source LLC
Chambersburg PA
CBHW051006050726
47592CB00007B/2734